ETSY

How To Turn Your Handmade
Hobby Into A Thriving Business

Table of Contents

INTRODUCTION

By picking up this e-book, you've probably already know about Etsy and you are probably interested in opening an Etsy shop but do not know where to being or don't know where to start. Etsy, it a great online platform that is a wonderful starting point to kick-start your fantastic hobby into a business because it opens you up to a whole new world ever-ready, buzzing marketplace with cool and easy to use interface that allows you to buy and sell with confidence.

Just last year, Etsy- the exciting and vibrant handmade marketplace celebrated their tenth year anniversary since their humble beginnings at a tiny apartment in Brooklyn. Since then, Etsy has created a mark for creative entrepreneurs, enabling them to connect with buyers and sellers, creating a unique environment that is known for niche, creative and most importantly- handmade.

Etsy, unlike Amazon's Handmade, goes far beyond just being a marketplace for creative entrepreneurs. It allows both buyer and seller to connect, discover various resources and attain stronger selling for their craft.

Etsy, doesn't mean anything right? Have you every wondered what is the meaning behind its name? Founder Rob Kalin in a Reader's Digest interview in 2010 said that he was looking for a name without any meaning, as he wanted to build the brand from scratch.

He said he was watching '8 ½' by celebrated director Federico Fellini and heard the actors uttering a word which sounded like 'Et Si.' Apparently, he said it meant 'Oh Yes!' in Italian.

Kalin actually misheard the actors because 'Oh yes' in Italian is "E Si", which when you think about it also can sound like Etsy, to us non-Italian speakers.

The name had a cutesy ring to it in English, and that's who Etsy came about.

CHAPTER 1
HISTORY OF ETSY

It's always good to learn a little more about a company's background history so in this chapter, we'll give you a brief history of Etsy. Over the last ten years, Etsy has grown into a 100$million dollar e-commerce company. It all started in 2005 when Haim Schoppik, Rob Kalin, and Chris Maguire created a company in their Brooklyn apartment. This company would give crafters and makers all around the world an online avenue to sell their wares.

Fast forward two years later; Etsy recorded 450,000 registered sellers as of 2007. This generated the company $26 million in annual sales and over $3 million in venture funding. Trouble cracked through for Etsy in 2008 when Maguire and Schoppick left the company due to a number of hours they were putting in to develop the business. Kalin, instead of letting go of the business, decided to recruit Chad Dickerson, who was at that time, senior director of products at Yahoo!. Dickerson joined Etsy as chief technology officer who took on the role swiftly and turned the company around. One of the key improvements was establishing Etsy's engineering team.

Dickerson's input into the company proved valuable since being hired at CTO. After three years, he became CEO, replacing Kalin. Kalin effectively left and removed himself from all management of the company. From this time onwards, Etsy made a significant shift- both in its culture as well as its corporate goals.

Dickerson then embarked on making the company more financially viable so in 2013, Etsy revamped in Terms of Service to enable sellers to sell manufactured goods as well as the handmade items. This became a stark contract from a company that was built around craftsmanship and supporting small business enterprises. The shift did not bode well with some crafters who wanted to leave the site, but it did not materialize because Etsy was affordable and it gave these crafters earning potential.

While there was a considerable outcry from the Etsy community, it did not cause a huge dent in the company's earning potential. Today, Etsy boasts 65 million users. The change in Terms of Service eventually helped the company to grow. Company sales from 2008 to 2015 increased steadily throughout the years. According to Statista, in 2013 alone, Etsy recorded sales from $895 million to $1.34 billion. In 2014, Etsy's revenue reached $195.6 million and in 2014, its gross merchandise sales peaked at $1.93 billion.

Apart from generating sustainable sales, Dickerson also made strategic moves such as hiring Mike Grishaver as senior vice president in July 2014- a bold move that earned the company some notice. Grishaver was originally from Pandora, a music streaming service where he served the same role as in Etsy. Etsy knew it needed to get onto consumer's mobile phones, so Ghrishaver joined in to develop Etsy's mobile component and form it into a mobile app for sellers.

Despite Etsy's move to become corporate, it has maintained its original foundation ideas. For example, Etsy has remained its status as a B-Corp business which means company values are stringent towards environmental and social standards. Compared to most businesses in the Silicon Valley, Etsy has maintained a much better employment statistic in terms of gender equality and diversity. It employs 51% female staffers in both leadership and tech teams. Facebook, by comparison only has 15% of women in tech or leadership roles. However, the company is 79% white.

By November 2015, Etsy has recorded 1.5 million active sellers with 22.6 million active buyers.

CHAPTER 2

CREATING YOUR SHOP, SIMPLE & EASY

Etsy has made it easy for anyone, anywhere to open up a shop. Since many of you are interested in opening up an Etsy shop, here's the ultimate step- by-step guide to open up your shop with a bang and start getting sales on the first listing!

A successful Etsy shop is a combination of several things- the right product, key actions and passion and you will be on your way of making much more than you original thought you could.

In this chapter, you will learn simple steps as well as a few key lessons.

TRUE STORY- HOW ONE SELLER TURNED $0.10 into $5,000

One Etsy seller shared her experience of how she started her Etsy shop. It all started with her wanting to include DIY ideas into her wedding- ideas that showcased both bride and groom. One of it was popcorn. This seller designed her very own popcorn bag and was online looking for Popcorn machine rentals. While browsing, she noticed that some other brides were looking for personalized popcorn bags.

In just a few moments, the seller downloads the Sell on Etsy app to her mobile phone and uploads a picture of her popcorn bag design. A week and a half go by, and she finally gets her first sale. After this, she customers her first design, uploads it and then a second and third sale rolled in. Within a mere four months, the seller high $5,000 from her shop.

How did she do it?

SETTING UP SHOP: THE ULTIMATE GUIDE TO SELLING ON ETSY

The process illustrated below is quite simple:

The flow stated above seems pretty straightforward and actually, it is. Is it quite simple right? Well… once you start thinking of a name and working on your logo, you might hit a few bumps and start stressing out. You have so many ideas, but you just don't know where to put them.

Before these little things get in the way and prevent you from featuring your first listing, here are a few easy tips to help you out:

STEP 1: NAMING YOUR SHOP

As with any business, giving it a name is one of the most exciting things! It gives your shop a look and feel and it also tells your customers what your shop sells. However, when you are in this step- don't obsess over it. Etsy gives you one chance to rename your shop, so the first tip is to name your store whatever that comes to your mind. Keep the name original, easy to pronounce and at the same time short and sweet- they are not only easier to remember, but it also helps with branding too.

STEP 2: DESIGNING YOUR SHOP

Another item to stop obsessing about your store design. Keep it basic, clean and fuss free- this is much better than having a messy, hard to navigate shop. Bear in mind that most buyers find your shop through Etsy's search engine so you would need to give more attention to the SEO part rather design. Progress is better than perfection so while you may not have a state of the art design, what is important is that you get the basics up first. Tweaking your site can come in later.

STEP 3: CREATING A LOGO

Just like your shop's name, your logo is equally important. If you have graphic design skills and can use photoshop and illustrator, then go for it and create your own logo. Otherwise, outsource your logo design to somebody who can. Speak to the designer and communicate your vision, your color choices, and your inspiration. Logo and branding go hand in hang so if this Etsy shop is something serious for you, focus on designing a logo that will appeal to your target market.

STEP 4: CREATING YOUR FIRST LISTING

Having a perfect name or the best logo will not give you any benefit until and unless you have listed your product. At this step, don't over-analyze things. In creating your first listing, here are a few steps to take:

a) Create a Prototype

What one of the biggest mistakes newbies make in their Etsy stores is making more than one test item even BEFORE they go live with their shop. The idea here is that they think they need several variations of listings on their items before starting. We are here to tell you that it'll create more problems and here's why:

- You do not need to impress potential buyers right away with so many choices. Buyers are at your site because they have something specific that they want- so give them that. No one else, except maybe your mom or your spouse and friends will look at every detail of your shop.

- Don't spend too much time creating an item with several colors or designs. Create just one prototype of the item and test and troubleshoot it.

- Try not to give our custom orders in your first listing. Shops that allow special orders will create a long line of special requests, and you would find yourself overwhelmed and underappreciated.

- Get something up and running- your trials and errors will eventually teach you how to right every wrong in your shop. So don't waste too much time or too much money trying to get your shop perfect. Procrastinating will end up with you not having a shop at all, an immense sense of self-doubt and fear.

STEP 5: TAKING PHOTOS

Photos are the first point of contact between your product and your customer. So believe it when we say that nobody is going to look at your design, logo or even name of your shop. Your customers got there because of the search engine. A client clicked on your photo because it was the most appealing to them. So the first thing that they will look at are:

1- Images of your listing
2- Pricing
3- Description of your product
4- Reviews
5- Store layout, design, logo
6- Shop Name.

Once you have your listing ready, get cracking on taking some good shots of your product. Nowadays, taking a good photo with even your smartphone is great- with a few little adjustments; you will have a great photo. However, once you have accumulated a small profit, it is a good idea to invest in a decent DSLR. We will cover photo taking tips in another chapter.

STEP 6: PUT ON THE PRICE TAG

Once you have a good set of product photos, time to set your pricing for each item. Determining how to price your items on Etsy can be difficult. That's why you need to do your market research. Check your competitors, check their pricing and products. See what sets you apart. You've probably come across advice saying to 'charge what you are worth' but if you are new to Etsy, and you do not have any sales experience, use these tips to help you determine your product 'worth':

1- How much did it cost to make your item?

At this step, you need to figure out what materials you used and how much it costs. For example, you plan on selling potted succulents:
Mini pots @ $3.50
Succulents @ $1.50
Cacti Soil @ $1.00/pot
Total: $6.00

2- How much are your upfront costs?

Do you have to buy equipment? Add in any design elements?

With the succulent example, you probably need to by some minor gardening tools or no tools at all. But you might need to get some proper packaging to ship this correctly. So let's say packaging costs $10.00 for a box and box fillers.

3- Costs to list Items:

Etsy charges $0.20 per listing. Listing is described as items for sale. Each listing costs your $0.20 but Etsy does not charge you 0.20 for every item you sell. But take note that a small portion minus off from your sale.

You can also get 40 free listings if you sign up as a seller through a referral from another vendor. You get 40 free listings, and the referral also gets 40 free listings.

4- Your Overall Total

With the three costing above, your overall total for one succulent is $16.20 (inclusive of your listing fee).

5- Your Time Costs

You must also include your time costs into the product pricing. How long did you take to do this? If one succulent took you an hour to put together, then how much of your time is it valued at? For example, if you want to make $10/hour, you need to add the material costs, upfront costs and fees to your time value. Professional makers and crafters charge $12 to $20 per hour.

A simple formula is:

Materials + Expenses + Labor/Workmanship + Profit = Wholesale x 2 = Retail

Alternatively, you can also use a calculator to help you cost your items. This is one such example: ETSY CALCULATOR.

STEP 7: STALK YOUR COMPETITORS

You just need to study your competitors to see what they are offering. How do their products differ from you? What are their prices?

As a new seller, you need to be competitive so perhaps you may need to price your item slightly lower than your established competitors. However, even if you didn't want to lower your prices from the market rate, you must then ensure that what you have is different and unique.

STEP 8: CREATING THE PERFECT DESCRIPTION

If writing isn't one of your strong components, then better get someone else to help you out and FAST! Writing descriptions can be a tedious task because let's face it- most Etsy stores sells a range of products under the same type. For example, if you sell earrings- you'd probably be selling studs, hoops, drop earrings, earrings findings and so on and so forth. While your product range may be vast, your product type remains the same and how many descriptions can we come up with before we run out of vocabulary?

So, get help from people around you. Your friends and family might come up with new ways of writing descriptions that can help you give a new approach to your products.

A few things to remember when writing descriptions:

1- keep it detailed. Tell your customers what it is, what it's made out of.

2- Take inspiration (but never plagiarize) from another seller's products.

3- Include keywords because it will help improve your listing

4- Tell your customers how soon can they expect delivery and if there are any customizations available.

STEP 9: CATCHING YOUR FIRST SALE

You've got your logo on fleek, your shop on point, your pictures popping and your product descriptions working. And now.... We wait.

Well..... sort of.

Getting your first sale is an exhilarating feeling! You achieved a milestone! You can do two things right now, which is:

1- Sit and wait for the sales to come in, which no doubt will take some time.

2- Do something about increasing sales!

If you have chosen option 2, then what you need to do now is track interest and test out different scenarios until you've found your eureka moment!

Option 1 is great if your Etsy shop is your side business but if you really want to quit your day job and focus on starting your own thing, being your own boss and doing what you love- then it's going to take a lot of hard work.

Some people get lucky- they get their first sale within a week of their listing. Some people are even more fortunate that they get a second or third sale while the first is being shipped out.

But instead of waiting it out for sales to come to your doorstep, take a proactive stance and do this instead:

1- Track your shop

Create a spreadsheet to track your shops' activity. Record how many views and favorites your listings get, what kind of listings get clicked on more, what keywords did you use?. All these things give you an idea what sells and what doesn't.

Tracking your shops' visitors activity will give you a good understanding of what needs to be revamped or tweaked- it could be your keywords, it could be your photos, it can even be your descriptions. For example, if one person has favorited your item from 100 views each day, but no sale has been made that means your keywords are excellent but you need to work on your photos or even your description.

Also, if many people have favorited your item but still no sale, it could mean that your keywords and pictures are great, but the pricing and description are what needs to be tweaked. This is what we mean by testing different scenarios. Change the pricing for an item by 10%- test it out for a week and if you haven't had any sales, then change your descriptions.

STEP 10: ADVERTISING OR SPONSORING YOUR LISTING

Honestly, it's always good to start out in generic terms to see how well customers receive your products on Etsy. However, different people have different approaches to increasing sales, and one of it is advertising.

In Etsy, there are many ways that you can do this:

You could:

- Open a Facebook page for your shop and pay for promo Facebook post that links back to your shop
- Pay directly in Etsy to promote the items to show up above the rest of the "like" items
- Create Google ads for your listing

STEP 11: GO FORTH AND PROSPER

Etsy isn't rocket science. In fact, anyone can create a successful side business in Etsy by being consistent, learning and reinventing and having passion.

The best part of having your own Etsy shop is that you can choose to grow it as much as you want and have fun doing what you like, while making money on the side.

If for instance you do not feel like selling at a particular time in Etsy, Etsy also has a vacation mode. You can set it on vacation mode for however long you need and not worry about the shop. Once you are ready again to come back on, reset to active mode.

Etsy has become a useful platform especially for stay-at-home moms who want to keep doing something, have income coming but at the same time be at home with their kids. Ten years ago, before the internet came along, this would not have been possible.

In the next few chapters, we will be covering more tips and tricks, formulas as well as some myths on Etsy.

8 THINGS TO THINK ABOUT WHEN OPENING AN ETSY SHOP

Sure, opening an account with Etsy is easy. The hard part would be what it's going to be called, what's in the name, what you are going to sell and so on. Here are some basic things to think about before you open an Etsy shop:

#1 What Can You Create?

You may be amazing at so many DIY things, but the thing is, does it sell? If you already have a hobby that you invest a lot of time and energy in, then this question is easy. A lot of people on Etsy already have something going on for them, even before Etsy came onto the internet of things, so with Etsy, it was just migrating their store into an online platform.

Whatever your interests are, there is always the possibility of taking your creativity to the next level by sharing what you love to the whole world. Take your time to think but to be honest with you; the fact that you are reading this e-book is already an indication of the fact that you already have an idea of what you want to do. You can sell almost anything on Etsy as long as it's handmade or vintage items and craft supplies.

#2 Get Your Market Research Done

As in every business, having a good foundation on what you are up against is always a good start. Doing market research will help you identify who your target customers are and if there's a market for your product. Even more so, you can also identify if Etsy is the best online platform for your product. Market research also gives you a firm understanding of who your competitors are and what are the current selling trends.

#3 Get your Inventory Done

You need to have products that are ready to sell. So one of the things you must think about is what kind of items you'd like to feature and sell in your shop. Spend extra time and thought into planning and creating a list of initial products that will give customers a clear insight of what you do, what your brand represents, your quality of work, capabilities and also build enticement and anticipation! First impressions matter so make it right!

#4 Work on your logistics

It's super easy to open an Etsy store, but what sets a successful store against a failed store is planning because, there are a lot of details that go into planning and organizing your store. These are just some of the few basic things to plan out:

a) Your Shop's Name – Brainstorm for exciting names because it tells people who you are. Choose carefully because Esty allows you to change your store's name only once.

b) Photos & descriptions- In the midst of creating your premier list, you must also work on getting some high-quality photographs. You want something that can immediately grab your viewer's attention and also show the audience what the product is about. Also, create a good description to go with the photos. Attractive and bright photos with a detailed description will increase sales.

c) Packing and Shipping- part of opening your shop is thinking about how you will pack and ship them and to which countries. Knowing the cost of packing and shipping is important in the planning stages, so you know how much to charge your customers. Not only that, a carefully packed package will arrive beautifully at your customer's doorstep, providing you with good reviews and make them buy from you again!

CHAPTER 3
INSIDER TIPS TO INCREASE SALES ON ETSY

Setting up a business can be daunting whether it is a brick and stone shop or online business. The good thing about setting up an online based store is that it requires minimal effort and more importantly, minimal investment. The risks involved in online businesses are not as significant as conventional stores.

Now that we've gone through the steps needed to open up an Etsy store, in this chapter, you will be learning some insider tips to increase your sales. Who doesn't want to increase their Etsy sales right?

Trust us, once you open your store- you'd want to sell, sell and sell! Nobody wants to start something and see it fail, and if you think about it, a successful business requires persistence and passion, with a little help from marketing tools, business acumen and well, luck. The thing is, it just isn't enough to open an Etsy shop and wait for customers to show up, browse and order your products. Even when it comes to conventional mortar & brick shops, you need to do some form of marketing.

While some find selling on Etsy easy, especially for those with sales experience. But for the rest of us, selling on Etsy needs some dedication, some time and some practice to figure things out. To stand out and increase sales, you need to be a savvy marketer. So if you want to take your Etsy business to the next level, it's time to look at things seriously. Here are some various tried and tested methods that you can employ to drive sales. Let's get started!

TIP #1: KNOW YOUR MARKET

Understanding your market is a major step in getting more sales. So ask yourself these questions:

- Who will buy your products?
- What are their needs?
- What are their problems?

Asking these questions will enable you to identify your niche market. Once you can figure out your ideal customer, you can start making strategic changes to market your product.

TIP #2: CREATE CATEGORIES

Categorizing your product gives it a specification. When classifying your product, identify what type of product it is. Is it material? Is it jewelry? Is it furniture? Is it decoration? Once you have created your categories, use the 'Shop Sections' in Etsy to organize your categories. This not only makes it easier for you, but it also makes it easier for your customers to shop!

TIP #3: BRANDING

Branding always helps any business to stay fresh and on top of a consumer's mind. Once you have opened your shop and started selling, in a few weeks, you will better understand how receptive your store is to your customers. Before you go into booming sales, make sure you have your branding on point. Pick a look and color scheme that makes customers acquaint this image to your store. Stay with a consistent signature logo and color scheme. When listing your products, keep it consistent too- they way you angle it, the background of the photo, the filters you use and so on need to be consistent.

Everything in your store needs to be consistent to be memorable in your clientele's mind.

TIP #4- OPTIMIZE WITH KEYWORDS

Optimizing your shop with keywords is essential as it will ensure you pop up in customers' search results via Etsy or via Google. So how do you do this? Essentially, there are three main sectors you need to optimize your shop:

1- SHOP TITLE: Use specific keywords in your shop title. The little area underneath your shop name is your shop title. Use keywords that describe your business or product. For example, The PinkLilyPress has a shop title that says "Wedding & Event Invitations, Stationery. Address Stamps" whereas the The Glocky Coggler's shop title is "Vintage. Victorian. Steampunk. Geek. Fantasy".

2- SHOP ANNOUNCEMENT: Your shop announcement is also an ideal place to incorporate SEO rich keywords! So don't for-go it.

3- SECTIONS: Concise and clear words in your product description also enhance your SEO. Make it easy for people to find you with just a few types of a keyword.

A good way to understand what your target market wants, use GOOGLE ADWORDS KEYWORD PLANNER. This planner enables you to identify what kind of words your clientele uses to search for products in your niche. Etsy also allows you to find out keywords phrases. Say for example you are selling 'Wedding Shower' products. To identify what keywords are used, do a quick search and type in 'Wedding Shower" and from there, you can see a list of keywords that buyers normally use to find what they want. Mix and match keywords but do not spam! Just like how you should not hashtag your Instagram pictures too much, adding unnecessary keywords to a listing will cause more harm.

TIP #5: PROVIDE STELLAR CUSTOMER SERVICE

If keywords and photos brought you, potential customers, outstanding customer service is what brings in return customers, referrals, positive reviews and repeat business. Answer questions as soon as you can, comment politely and promptly, offer discounts, and most importantly fast shipping is what will make customers satisfied.

TIP #6: SET COMPETITIVE PRICES

Give yourself some time to see how your shop relates and reacts to your audience. During the initial few months of your shop, keep your shop's pricing similar to the market rate or slightly lower. Review your prices every 3 to 6 months to see how it reacts to customers. Often, lowering costs isn't the only solution. What you can do is to try to cut costs but increase the value of your product- such as offering better packaging, better photographs and so on.

TIP #7: COLLABORATE

Nowadays, collaboration is key to a successful business. You've heard the saying "Two heads are better than one, right?" Same thing goes for selling on Etsy. What are other sellers doing that I'm not doing? Sometimes, you can also look outside Etsy to see how other brands increase sales. How about collaborate?

If you want to increase sales, collaborate with a local artist or talent or crafter from Etsy itself to produce products that are one of a kind. Bloggers do this all the time! They invite other bloggers to write guest- posts. Collaboration across various elements will not only help sales, but it will also give you a wider appeal. Collaboration also brings about new ideas, and it also brings two different interest groups to purchase your products.

TIP #11: LEARN HOW TO PHOTOGRAPH BETTER

Visual identities are always more clickable. Customers cannot touch and feel your product, so the best way that they can see what you offer is through the images you have. Since opening your shop, investing in some photo editing program and a good camera is essential. If you already have a camera, then install programs like Adobe Photoshop or Lightroom. These programs can help you clean, enhance and refine your images.

TIP #12: KEEP ON ADDING LISTINGS

Listings help you get found on Etsy. Adding more and more items on a frequent basis keeps your customers interested in your shop. Variety offered on your store also increases the chances of a customer buying your product.

TIP #13: SUPPORT A SOCIAL CAUSE

Whenever there is a holiday around the corner or a celebration like Christmas or Mother's Day, most if not all, Etsy stores tailor their product offering to meet the demands of the holiday season. This is a usual practice. To go one step further, why not offer products that support a social cause of your choice? For example, if you support LGBT rights, then either create a product that would make customers buy it in support of the cause OR let customers know that a percentage of their purchase will go as a donation to a cause.

TIP #14: HAVE A SEASONAL SALE

Shopping malls do it so why can't you? Every once or twice a year plan a seasonal sale that allows your clientele to purchase items at discounted rates and in bulks. This not only helps increase views to your site, but it also clears out items that have a slower selling rate and gives you a fresh start to introduce new products to your store.

TIP #15: BE ACTIVE ON SOCIAL MEDIA

This is no excuse. If you have an online shop- you have got to be active on social media. Being connected on various social media platforms increases your publicity because you connect to different users. Depending on what you sell and what your customer's interests are, they will be hanging out in different social Medias. The most common social media accounts are Pinterest, Facebook, Instagram, and Twitter. But then there's also talent or hobby-centric sites like DeviantArt, Flickr, and Tumblr that serve a niche group. So if you provide design elements or typefaces, fonts or designs- DeviantArt is an excellent choice to be on. If you sell photography related items, the Flickr is great.

TIP #16: BLOG AROUND YOUR BRAND

If you set up shop, then set up a blog! A blog is an excellent way to convey what you are like a shop, share your thoughts and ideas and build your credibility. You can blog about anything but remember to tie it to your shop. For instance, if there is an article on ethical fashion and if your brand does ethical or organic clothing, then write about this article and connect some keywords to your shop.

TIP #17: ASK FOR REVIEWS

After looking at pricing and product description, customers look at reviews next. Reviews are crucial for online businesses because it tells buyers how good of a seller you are. Good reviews generate sales as people find you trustworthy. To encourage reviews, ask your customers politely. Create a template to use to send them in an email. Here's a sample that you can use:

"Hello ___!
Thank you for purchasing from my store ___. Hope you like it!
Your feedback will help so much in improving my store.
You can add your review here: www.etsy.com/your/purchases.

Thank you so much for your time!

Yours Truly,

_____

TIP #18: PARTICIPATE IN FAIRS, MARKETS, AND EXPOS

By participating in fairs, markets and expos, you exponentially increase your virtual presence. It is also a great way to meet like-minded people, share knowledge as well as learn more about your craft, about growing your business and also inspire and be inspired. Promote your various engagements on your blog and social media and invite your customers to meet you. Have a goodie bag ready for them to take away when they visit your booth, discount your products and take as many wefies and selfies to upload on your social media sites.

TIP #19: BUY ADVERTISEMENTS

Some Etsy stores face very stiff competition such as for items like jewelry and home furnishing. So if you are in this niche, then consider purchasing paid posts or advertisements to broadcast your products. You can also take advantage of Etsy's promoted listings which make it easy to list your product. Of course, then there's Facebook's advertising to get on to as well.

TIP #20: NETWORK WITH OTHER SELLERS

Connecting and contacting other sellers is a great way to get ahead. You can get more tips, share ideas and even bundle your products together to attract new customers.

Wrapping Up!

While there isn't a magic solution to get sales into your shop, there are strategic marketing techniques that you can use to plan and execute your campaign. All it takes is a little homework and getting the basics right first. Always remember to get to know your target audience first then build a good brand.

CHAPTER 4

USING SOCIAL MEDIA TO DRIVE SALES

Marketing on Social Media is part of establishing and making your Etsy business robust. Because there are so many social media platforms out there, a plan is always good to identify what works and what doesn't and also where you fans are most likely to hang out in and what interests them on social media.

In this chapter, we will discuss some effective social media strategies that you can employ for an Etsy Store:

STRATEGY #1- CONSTRUCT A PLAN

Everything you set out to do, must have a plan. The same goes for your social media strategies to push your Etsy store to the online universe. In developing your plan, make sure you know your amount of free time and resources. Consider how much commitment you are planning on giving to your Etsy site. Do you want it to become big enough to enable you to quit your job? Or do you want it only as a side hustle? If your plans are big, your social media strategies should be more prominent. Plan which sites you want paid advertising and which sites should be free. Decided how you would like to use each of these sites.

For example:

Instagram- FREE. To post updates on project processes and upcoming projects. Put up previews or appearances.

Facebook- PAID. Take advantage of paid advertising by reaching out to millions all across the globe.

Tumble- FREE. Connect with other Etsy sellers. Post inspirational quotes.

Pinterest- PAID. Promote your Etsy store through BUYABLE PINS!

Twitter- FREE. Follow celebrities, connect with your customers. Post and repost!

STRATEGY #2- BE SPECIFIC ABOUT WHAT YOU WANT

With your Etsy shop set up, develop a set of targets you want to achieve with it so that it goes on seamlessly with your social media plans. Develop precise, measurable and attainable objectives. For example, your goals for your shop can be:

1. Sell 200 scarves by October 15.
2. Sell 500 sweaters by October 30.
3. Sell 130 blue leg warmers by October 12.
4. Make 220 yellow mittens by October 30
5. Make $1000 in profits/month by November 30.
6. Make $1950 in profits/month by December 31.
7. Spend 30minutes/day exercising

Your objectives will be more different than this, but this is just an example. These goals give you accurate dates and figures so you can always challenge yourself to achieve these measurable objectives.

STRATEGY #3- CHOOSE YOUR PLATFORMS WISELY

There are a dozen of social media platforms that you can usw, to find your specific customers:

On Etsy itself you can also find many sellers you can easily connect with. If you are a crafter, open an Etsy store.

Facebook is really the best social media site for your Etsy Business. Almost everyone has Facebook, and it would be a waste if you didn't have a Facebook Business Page.

Pinterest provides a marvelous way to market your crafts visually. You can inspire and be inspired.

Twitter is a excellent to reach target niche markets, in particular through hashtags.

YouTube or Vimeo provide a lot of opportunities to connect to your potential buyer through videos

Google+ can great for connecting with with other people or organizing Video Hangouts.

With social media, there is one important point to consider. What you want to do is to focus your efforts and narrow them down on a few sites so you can gain success with two or three social media platforms.

When starting out your social media strategy, start with a site that you are familiar with. From then on, you develop your self-confidence and skills and then you can try testing other social media sites.

Facebook is a great site to begin with. You probably already have a personal profile account, so all you need to do now is create a Facebook Page to market your Etsy Shop. Make sure you use the same concept, design, logo, name and color theme for your Facebook page. Remember, consistency is key.

STRATEGY #4: FACEBOOK MARKETING

Firstly, set up your Business Facebook page! And it's very straightforward really. Having a business page for your Etsy shop makes things more trustworthy, and there are many more ways you can market your store via your Facebook page.

As with Etsy, having visuals for your Facebook page does wonders. Use your cover page wisely. You can upload images of new products, you can upload a fair/trade expo that you are planning to attend, you can upload anything that relates to your business. Keep your business profile picture the same, though- keep your logo on it. ALWAYS.

When setting up your profile page, don't forget to include your Etsy shop link, your website and also sync your other social media sites such as Twitter and Tumblr and your blog on it.

If you didn't already know, you could integrate your Etsy shop with your Facebook page too! It isn't very hard to do either. All you need to do is install an app such as WishPond. Log into your account on Etsy and install Whishpond for your Etsy Facebook Store. Follow the instructions on your screen and just like that, you have created your Etsy store on your Facebook page. The Etsy for Facebook will appear as a tab within your Page, and you can create your custom page as you wish to.

Once you have done this, you can now include content. This should be fairly easy because all you need to do is copy the content from your Etsy site. Again, consistency is key.

When posting on Facebook, you can include various news items from your product updates, images, how-tos and even share updates on your industry, what other sellers are up to, lifestyle tips and also customer testimonials.

STRATEGY #5- USE HASHTAGS

You probably already know what hashtagging, and hashtags are. Almost all social media available today uses hashtags, even Facebook. Hashtagging is an excellent way to share your posts and get it liked and followed by as many people as you can.

Here's why you should be using a hashtag:

- Hashtagging allows you to become part of a large discussion within your specific niche.
- You can use it to market your crafts by riding on a trending hashtag
- A unique hashtag piques interest in your marketing campaigns and even your Etsy shop. For example, if your Shop's name is Rock & Gold, then you can create a hashtag like #dressuprockandgold

STRATEGY #6- UTILIZE FACEBOOK TABS

Another great social site to link with your Facebook would be Pinterest. Include Twitter or your own Blog too. On your Facebook page, upload videos and tutorials. Don't make your Etsy store and your products the only information on your page. Give variety in your postings to keep different people interested.

STRATEGY #7- TRACK & MEASURE

You've put in a considerable amount of time, energy and money. So the need to track what you have done so far to see how it is working is imperative. Marketing strategies must be tracked and results recorded. Measure your results such as the numbers of likes you've received since paying for Facebook ads, the number of shares, views and fans as well as how many clicks received to your shop through Facebook.

The bottom line is, start with something familiar. You may be very familiar with using Twitter or Instagram but not so much on Facebook so strategize according to what you are comfortable with.

There are plenty of entrepreneurs who started out with only an Instagram account while some with Youtube accounts. Some, until now have chosen to stick to only one social media account. So that is entirely up to you.

Having too many accounts and not utilizing it to its fullest potential is just a waste of time for you. So best to stick the ones you know.

USING PINTEREST TO PROMOTE ETSY

Just like Facebook Page, Pinterest also requires you to open an account specifically for your business. You can do this by either converting your existing persona account into a business account OR you might just need to open a brand new business account. Do whichever that works for you.

To convert or create a new account, visit http://business.pinterest.com.

Your Pinterest for Business account will be able to give you Pinterest analytics your personal account can't. This means you can tell whether or not your marketing efforts to promote your business is working or not.

So once you are done with that, here come the next steps:

#1 CREATE BOARDS RELATED TO YOUR PRODUCT/BUSINESS

Firstly, create at least five business-related boards on your Pinterest Business account. Create boards that are related to the products you sell and the brand you have created. You can also have a board that is dedicated to all the posts you have on your blog site or one board for all your Etsy products. There can also be one board showing behind the scenes. One online shop- The Perfect Palette regularly features boards with color inspiration.

#2 CHOOSE WORDS THAT RELATE TO YOUR BUSINESS

Again, keywords and hashtags are useful. So with Pinterest, use keywords that are relevant to your boards. Think about the terms that people use if they were searching for something to do that is related to the business that you do or the products that you sell. Also, get creative with your board names. Try to stay away from Generic titles such as 'My Products' or 'My Blog Posts'. Nobody is going to type in 'my blog posts' to find something that they want. One pinner features her boards as

29

'Work That Body!' (for workouts) 'Fuel That Body' (for food and recipes) which is creative and eye-catching. Use relevant keywords. For example, if you sell jewelry, you can name your boards 'Sparkling Neck Accessories' or even 'Sparkling Ring Things'. Jazz up your words but also keep in mind to not make it confusing.

After your 5 business boards, create another 5 that is not directly related to your business, but it still has some form of connection to your niche or industry. For example, you can have boards related to Etsy photography, Inspirational and motivational quotes, fashion, productivity, organization and so on.

So essentially, you want at least 5 boards related to what you do and 5 that aren't directly related but still support the primary business.

#3 PIN, PIN AND PIN

Like every other social media account out there, posting, linking and pinning regularly is imperative to promoting your craft business. Frequency and consistency keep your followers aware of your existence. Unlike other social media, Pinterest creates the ability to engage followers by sharing interests. People will pin back what you have pinned if they like your pin and find it useful to keep in their boards. Do not pop in once a week and the go on a Pinning rage- you will be spammy, and people might unfollow you because you are flooding their news feeds. Be smart- share relevant content a few days at a time-space out your posts because it isn't useful to pin things every day.

#4 VARIETY

Again, don't make your posts or your business or your products the only thing you pin about. You will lose followers faster than a lightning strike. On a daily basis, stick to pinning about 5 pins. Also, pin a mixture of content.

Some rules to follow when pinning:

1- Try to space out. Pin two days once.

2- Have a ratio of at least 60% other content and 40% your content

3- Pin to-do, hacks, DIYs, quotes as well as business articles that you can find on the net which you may feel useful to read

4- Podcasts and videos are also helpful. This can be from your site as well as from other sites.

Pinterest is really addictive, and you can spend hours on it to read things, learn about stuff and find out what other people are interested in.

PLATFORM	MON	TUES	WED	THURS	FRI	SAT	SUN
BLOG	Post tutorial & Promote Give-Away	-	-	Promote Give-Away	-	Post your own article about Met Gala inspirations for upcoming designs	REST
TWITTER	Link blog post	Repost Content from DeviantArt	MET GALA Today! Post Claire Danes outfit #metgala 2016	-	Repost content on Give-Away	Link blog post	REST
INSTAGRAM	Post Give-away Promo		Post on #metgala2016	-	-	Post specific image from blog post	REST
FACEBOOK	Link Blog Post	Share link from other craft blog	Post on #metgala2016	Share link on news item from Craftiviti!	-	Link blog post	REST

SOCIAL MEDIA PLANNER

It's good to plan out your social media assault. Here is a sample of a Weekly Social Media plan that you can follow to pin, post, share and link on all your various Social Media accounts. This planner shows that not every day has a to-do- sometimes, less is more.

5 Ways Etsy Sellers Get Social Media Wrong

Social media is no doubt the place to promote products and services and to connect with customers. Every sphere of business has a Facebook account- even NonGovermental organizations and social enterprises. Social media gives businesses a direct relationship with their customers. So it doesn't matter so much of IF you have social media, it's more of a matter HOW WELL you do social media.

While there are many positive things about using social media, a wrong step could be a PR disaster that can leave a lasting negative impact and cause a massive drop in sales. Just as how fast word spreads if you do something amazing and post it up on social media, it can spread just as fast, if not faster, if you have done something wrong.

Here are five situations to consider when promoting your Etsy store on social media sites:

1- Incomplete Social Profiles

Opening up a social media account and not completing it with all the info is jut unprofessional. Having a well defined Facebook profile page, Twitter or Instagram will show your customers that you are downright serious. Never open an account and not have it completed with the right info.

2- You Don't have To be Everywhere

An Etsy shop, however easy they have made it for you to set it up on your own, does take time to list things, price it, photograph and so on. It's just like running a conventional brick store. So managing several different social media sites to keep your fan base updated will also take a considerable amount of time. Luckily for you, you do not need to at all your social media accounts 24 hours. It is all about picking the right social media for your site. Keep it to 2 or 3 sites so you don't spread yourself too thin.

3- Tailor Your Messages

Depending on what social media accounts you use, tailor make your messages. Some posts are worth to be shared on all your accounts whereas some are meant to be shared at specific sites. For example, Twitter is ideal for quick one line messages. Instagram has some limitations where it prevents you from including new links, so Instagram best works for quick video tutorials and for promo images. Facebook is great to repost news items from different sellers or from the industry. Sharing the same content on all your various social media over and over again might cause people to unfollow you or find you irritating.

4- Keep the Self Promotion Minimal

Pushing your products too much and too often is the quickest way to lose fans and followers. It is a lot of white noise to your followers when you just keep promoting your business and products. To make your business succeed and well-received, always inject variety into your posts so do different things to switch up your tempo so that you can inform and engage your fans all the time. Value and quality about quantity and white noise- remember that.

5- No Consistency

Well laid out and consistent posting is the key to long-term social media success. Keep your fans anticipating for what's new (that's why variety is always good). Create anticipation, create fervor and create interest with your postings.

CHAPTER 5
ESSENTIAL PHOTOGRAPHY TIPS FOR YOUR ETSY STORE

Visual identities create a look and feel for a business. People like to see photos and color and social media, blogs and websites that have interesting and captivating pictures attract attention a lot faster than a blog or website with all words and no images at all.

That said, photos are also easy to mess up your Etsy shop. Have you thought about that? While you may not do it on purpose, your photos may be the reason you aren't getting any sales. So in this chapter, we'll look a little bit in detail on how we can master the basics of how to get a good photo.

When you go onto Etsy as a buyer, think about how you respond to a sellers products. Chances are you clicked on a product with a nice photo, right?

You aren't alone. Almost everyone browsing on Etsy clicks on products that have great pictures. If you have pictures that are grainy, too dark or too light, blurry or out of focus, nobody is going to click on your pictures. And if no one clicks, it doesn't get sold.

Nobody cares if you have great items on your shop. Nobody will see it if they don't click on it. It also doesn't matter if your items are of fantastic quality- nobody will know if they don't see it.

It can be a little tricky to get the basics right if you are starting out in photography and you do not have any kind of professional photography. But fret not; getting good in photography just needs some time to get things right and then you are on the way to awesomeness. So do not feel bad that your pictures aren't professional level let. Instead, what you need to be is stay motivated to ensure you get enticing and beautiful photos.

6 Tips to Make Photography Easier

There are plenty of websites out there that have tips and tricks on how you can take amazing pictures and edit them to professional quality. Plus, photography technology has improved so much that it makes it so easy to work a camera.

Firstly, you do not need a really expensive camera. If you are low on budget, you can stick to your smartphone! iPhones are amazing when it comes to capturing beautiful pictures. But if you can, invest in a good DSLR or digital camera.

Secondly, you want to keep things simple. Look back at Etsy and take a look at the various pictures uploaded. If you notice, most pictures have these common traits:

1. Lots of natural light
2. Simple backgrounds
3. Detail, detail, detail
4. Angles Matter
5. Use the same setup
6. And then practice practice practice.

Let's break it down...

TIP #1: NATURAL LIGHT

Having a good dose of natural light is always excellent for photos. If your home does not have good natural light pouring in, then take your product outdoors. If you have lots of bright and natural light, pick a good spot and start snapping away. Alternatively, you can also invest in a good spotlight to brighten your images.

There are many tutorials online that teach you how you can create your own light box- it doesn't take long, and it is a super cost effective way to get perfect lighting with a clean background.

TIP #2: UNCOMPLICATED BACKGROUNDS

The focus of your photos should be your product. Not the environment, not the ambiance, not the scenery. It is your product that's the star of the show so keep it simple.

The Best Background for Beginners

If you notice most Etsy photos always have a white background. White backgrounds are excellent for two reasons:

1- White works for every skill level. It makes your products pop out, and you do not need to use props or any effects for a great photo. A white background is simple and easy to use, with minimal fuss.

2- A white background perfectly captures the product. It showcases every aspect of your product, giving buyers a good idea of the shape and color. Also, a white background enables the viewer to focus directly immediately on the product and nothing else.

So how do you get a white background? You can employ several different methods:

1- Use a white sheet

2- use a thick white cardboard or poster board- anything bigger than A3 words perfectly

3- Use a DIY light box. You Can find how to make one here.

Depending on what your product is, white backgrounds may not be suitable for everything. For example, if your product is bright or white, then use a contrasting background.

Sometimes, staging a product also works like a rug or pillows. If you sell earrings or bracelets or necklaces, then use a model or buy a jewelry display. In this way, you are giving the buyer an idea of context as well as size and dimension.

If you like to use a different background, that is totally fine, just remember to focus on your product.

TIP #3: IT IS ALL IN THE DETAILS

Think about how you look at things when you want to purchase a dress or a sweater or even a glass vase. When we go shopping, the good thing is we can pick the items up and examine them. We hold them, look at them, feel them and check for any damages.

This doesn't work the same for online shopping, unfortunately. Always remember that our customers cannot feel what we sell when we sell it online and the only way that they can judge a product is by its photos and of course a shop's reviews.

How do we ensure that our customers are able to get all the details they need to make a purchase? It's easy:

- Make sure your pictures are clear and features every aspect of your item in great detail
- Take far distance shots to give the bigger picture and close up shots to feature details
- Think of including an object to show perspective. Place the object next to another item to show dimensions
- Explain these particulars in the descriptions such as material, sizing, texture and so on.

TIP #4: ANGLES MATTER

Angles make your photos look professional. Angles determine the parts of your product that your customer most likely wants to see. Etsy allows you to upload up to 5 images per item so if your first photo shows the front of your product, show the back of the product, so they have an overall view of what you are selling. Remember to give your customers:

- The top,
- the back,
- the sides,
- the inside

Give them more access to the little details of your product to increase the likelihood of your customers clicking and checking out with your product.

Keep in mind though that not all products require a complete overview, for example, paintings so while you can give 5 different photographs of your painting, try to keep the focus with just maybe 3 looks of your painting. From afar, close up and maybe the frame that comes with the painting.

Clothing, bags, shoes, hats, dresses and furniture are items that buyers would want more details so all of these can be attained through featuring your product in different angles.

TIP #5: USE THE SAME SET

Once you've found a good spot for lighting and you had your perfect background and figured out your angles, you have gotten over the hard part. So since you have these items improved, don't stray. Use this same exact set up for all your photos because guess what- IT IS CONSISTENCY, AND CONSISTENCY IS KEY.

However, to spice things up, you can alternate between backgrounds and just add something different to a few photos, but there must always be some sense of similarity:

- Consistent background(s)
- Consistent natural lighting
- Consistent camera angles
- Consistent camera settings
- Consistent camera distance/zoom
- Same time of day so the shadows are at the same angle

Why do you need to have some sense of similarity? For these two reasons:

1. This means you can take photos fast and easily because you already have your set up, and you know exactly what to use and where to place your products to get the best lighting

2. You have a sense of consistency and continuity because things have the same look and feel, which contributes extensively to your branding

TIP #6: PRACTICE, PRACTICE, PRACTICE

You have definitely heard that practice makes perfect. With the perfect lighting perfect spot, knowing your angles and a good background, take your DSLR, digital camera or smartphone for a photo shooting extravaganza. Take loads and loads of photos because the more you take, the better you will understand how your camera works, how angles work, how lighting and shadow works and in no time, you'll be a pro at it.

What you can do is take small batches of the same product and then upload them to your computer. Sometimes, pictures look amazing on the camera screen, but it does not translate well on a computer screen. Your objective is to make sure that it looks great on a computer screen because that's what people will look on. Once you see the unedited images on your computer, you can then see what areas you need to tweak0 maybe lighting, maybe angle, etc. By taking several pictures of the same product, you can decide which shot perfectly showcases your product.

Once you are done with taking pictures, use a photo editing software such as Adobe Photoshop to enhance your images by working the contrast and brightness, color saturation, shadows, and highlight.

CHAPTER 6:

5 ETSY MYTHS THAT ARE RUINING YOUR BUSINESS

You've probably by now read all there is to know about opening up a store on Etsy. It is no doubt a great place to get a kick start in your craft career. With technology and the internet, there is nothing that is not within our reach these days and we can utilize all the tools out there to make a living.

While there's a lot of advice on opening up an Etsy store, does and don'ts, tips, and tricks, there are also some myths that might be ruining your store and killing your sales!

In this chapter, we will look at some facts and dispel any myths associated with running your Etsy shop.

Firstly, before we go on to the myths, here is some advice to follow:

Always fact check. When you are out seeking advice for your business, do yourself a favor and fact check two important factors:

1. Is your advice source in any business and has she or he sold any kind of physical product online?
2. Does your advice giver have a successful online shop or business that has proven sales records?

Sometimes, people just dispense advice without even having any experience (like how keyboard warriors give advice on parenting when they aren't even parents!).

Save yourself time and effort and speak to people who are real experts in their industry and it doesn't have to be Richard Branson (although you can follow him on LinkedIn to get inspiration and read his articles).

It can be any home-based or work-from-home individual to whom you are closely acquainted with. Speak to them, pick their brains out and get a first-hand story about how they started and the challenges they went through.

Keep in mind though that some advice may contradict with your own understanding of how to run things. Again, it's like parenting. What you do might be wrong to someone and what another person does may not work for you.

The point here is to learn different ways of doing things. Be open to suggestions but always use your common sense and instinct.

That said, here are some myths we will dispel about Etsy and your Etsy shop:

MYTH #1: CREATE AS MANY OPTIONS AND LISTINGS AS POSSIBLE. IT WILL GET YOU MORE SALES.

As mentioned in earlier chapters, don't create any options for customization especially when you are still learning how to sell on Etsy. More options and customization doesn't necessarily translate to higher sales because it will overwhelm you especially when you are not ready. Choices and customization will only interrupt the process of buying and selling. Most people shopping on Etsy want a 'get in, get out' fuss-free shopping experience so give them that. You also do not want to delay their shopping experience with customization because it will also overwhelm them.

This rule here doesn't apply to all products. Some products benefit from customization such as for engraving jewelry, customizing t-shirts and so on. But our advice for first time Etsy shop owners- give yourself some time do conduct normal business before providing customization.

MYTH #2: CUSTOMERS LOVE YOUR HANDMADE STORY

Claude Hopkins in the Scientific Advertising journal in the 1920s said this about a client's buying process:

"Remember the people you address are selfish, as we all are. They care nothing about your interests or your profit. They seek service for themselves. Ignoring this fact is a common mistake and a costly mistake in advertising. Ads say in effect, 'Buy my brand. Give me the trade you give to others. Let me have the money.' This is not a popular appeal."

Unless the person visiting your site is a journalist and needs to write a story about your Etsy success, nobody is going to care how you started off. The thing is, writing about your journey in handmade craft is useful to Etsy as a marketing brand because that's what Etsy is all about- a Handmade Marketplace. But the customer doesn't care. All they care about 'What's in it for me?'.

When writing your ABOUT PAGE, keep it simple. Nobody's going to read about you unless they have a greater interest in your products and have been a loyal customer for awhile. Write your About page for your customer, not for yourself. Here are some examples:

1- Adding Product Links to Create Ideas

Hi there! The things in this shop are meant to provide accent pieces for any home. Turn a boring chaise lounge into a statement piece with my hand knitted Afghan drape or create a focal point in your house with this fantastic chevron throw rug. You can a find all these and more on my shop. Happy Shopping!

2- Short and Simple Intro

I am a work at home mom! Between juggling my day job as an accountant and being a mother, crafting sterling jewelry keeps me sane. Jewelry pieces featured in my shop are designed and created by me with inspiration from nature, my babies, and life.

3- Seller's own experience with wanting something different

I have always liked dragon motive jewelry but for some reason, it's hard to find something I truly like. The dragon-inspired jewelry you see here is a creation of my own designs. It's meant to be chic, stylish yet edgy.

MYTH #3- STUFF YOUR TITLES FOR BETTER SEO

Stuffing keywords into your storefront is a recipe for disaster. If you have done it, did you see any changes in your sales? Did it get you to the top of the list?

If someone told you that to get more views, you had to make your storefront keyword dense is actually setting you up for failure. Stats count, but too much of something is never good. At the end of the day, although your statistics and number of views increase but your sales don't, then this marketing concept has failed you.

If there were a sure-fire way of getting your Etsy page seen easily, everyone would be doing it. Sadly, there isn't. Etsy, just like Facebook and even Instagram changes their coding and algorithms regularly. Want prove? Read ETSY's CEO Chad Dickerson's interview here.

In getting good views, don't just rely on Etsy traffic. You are setting up shop where there's 22.6 million active buyers. So think outside the box and find ways of reaching out to new customers OUTSIDE of Etsy. As mentioned earlier on, you can do this easily view social media.

MYTH #4- USE MAGIC KEYWORDS

While it is true that keywords help you get to the top of the SEO ranking, there's so much more that you can do to get to the top.

This tip is from one Etsy seller:

Attract customers everywhere on the web and direct them to the location of your site. To do this, write blog posts, write guest blog posts, use Facebook Ads, Pinterest Business pages and even Instagram sponsored ads. This will increase your online presence and also connect with like-minded people.

Doing all these different things and using all the various online tools can help you get the sales you want, instead of overdoing your keywords.

In the land of SEO, using online tools and platforms increases your backlinks. Technically speaking, the number of backlinks a website has shows the popularity of that website on the internet. The more popular a website, the higher it will be on a Google search.

Just take note that none of this happens overnight or immediately after you've paid your Facebook ad. This also takes time.

A combination of sensible keywords and magnificent marketing strategy is what will get you to the top. But like all things, it takes time too.

MYTH #5: YOU CANT BUILD AN EMAIL LIST FROM YOUR ETSY SALES

When you make a sale on Etsy, that customer is yours. Always remember that Etsy just hosts your store, but they cannot claim every customer as their own. They aren't the ones doing the designing, the marketing, the packaging or the shipping- it's you!

You have every right in the world as a seller to connect and contact your customer after they have made a purchase. After all, it is excellent customer service to ask them how they feel shopping with you. Their feedback can really help you.

So essentially, it isn't illegal to build your list. But to make all things fair, ask your customers if they would like to be part of your mailing list. After all, Etsy does have one on its own, so why not you.

Under the CAN-SPAM Act, there are SEVEN RULES that you must abide by when using email platforms such as MailChimp to connect with your customers. So just don't break any of these rules, and you are ready to go!

CONCLUSION

Starting your side business or quitting your job and turning into a full-time online entrepreneur has never been so easy with Etsy. Anyone from anywhere in the world can become sellers by providing handmade, vintage items. Etsy has given many people, especially stay-at-home moms to earn a living. People like Alicia Bock, Janick Gravel, Heather Moore and Nafsika Kokkini have all created successful Etsy stores and made a living out of it.

Etsy has also opened up doors for crafters, artists and designers to reach new audiences from all around the globe.

Hopefully, this book has managed to cover all the essential details of opening up your very own Etsy store and has given readers insider tips and tricks to help them get a kick-start in opening up their store without a hitch. As with everything else, trial and error is always a great way to learn and to understand your store and improve on things.

Use whatever tips and tricks that come by your way but always remember to check back, calculate and track your store's performance so you know whether what you are doing is worth it and bringing in the numbers that you want.

What are you waiting for? Get your Etsy store up now!